T
CH_____ ___ _____

*"For there is no power
but from God."*
         —Romans 13:1

THE REIGN OF CHRIST THE KING

By

Michael Davies

"For the Lord is our judge, the Lord is our lawgiver, the Lord is our king."

—Isaias 33:22

TAN BOOKS AND PUBLISHERS, INC.
Rockford, Illinois 61105

Library of Congress Catalog Card No: 92-61180

ISBN: 0-89555-474-7

Printed and bound in the United States of America.

TAN BOOKS AND PUBLISHERS, INC.
P.O. Box 424
Rockford, Illinois 61105
1992

"Pilate therefore said to him: Art thou a king then? Jesus answered: Thou sayest that I am a king. For this was I born, and for this came I into the world."

—John 18:37

CONTENTS

This book is a slightly adapted version of a talk given by Michael Davies at the VNI Conference in the Chicago area in November of 1991. VNI—Voice Network International—is an organization based in the Chicago area and run by Catholic laymen to promote solid Catholic restoration in the Church.

THE REIGN OF
CHRIST THE KING

On 11 December 1925 Pope Pius XI promulgated his encyclical letter *Quas Primas,* on the Kingship of Christ. The encyclical dealt with what the Pope described correctly as "the chief cause of the difficulties under which mankind was laboring."

Pope Pius XI explained that the manifold evils in the world are due to the fact that the majority of men have thrust Jesus Christ and His holy law out of their lives; that Our Lord and His holy law have no place either in private life or in politics; and, as long as individuals and states refuse to submit to the rule of our Saviour, there will be no hope of lasting peace among nations. Men must look for the peace of Christ in the Kingdom of Christ—*Pax Christi in Regno Christi.*

CHRIST'S KINGSHIP IGNORED IN THE CHURCH?

In the February, 1976 issue of *Approaches,* Hamish Fraser stated with, alas, complete accuracy, that *Quas Primas* is virtually ignored by the so-called Catholic nations and by the Catholic clergy. It was, he lamented, the greatest non-event in the entire history of the Church.

What is it that caused the Catholic clergy, and the bishops of the world in particular, to be so embarrassed by this encyclical that it was virtually ignored at the time of its promulgation, and has been all but forgotten in the post-Vatican-II epoch? What is it about this encyclical which caused its teaching to be passed over in silence, if not actually contradicted, by the Second Vatican Council? It is an incontrovertible fact that this Council conspicuously and, one must conclude, deliberately, failed to reaffirm the teaching of *Quas Primas*.

THE UNIVERSAL RIGHTS OF CHRIST

The answer to these questions is that in this encyclical Pope Pius XI reaffirmed the unbroken teaching of his predecessors upon the papal throne that *states* as well as individuals must submit themselves to the rule of Christ the King. In affirming this fundamental truth of our faith, Pope Pius was not referring simply to Catholic nations, or even to Christian nations, but to the whole of mankind. He stated this truth unequivocally by quoting a passage from the encyclical *Annum Sacrum* of Pope Leo XIII:

> The empire of Christ the King includes not only Catholic nations, not only baptized persons who, though of right belonging to the Church, have been led astray by error, or have been cut off from her by schism, but also all those who are outside the Christian faith; so

that truly the whole of mankind is subject to
the power of Jesus Christ.

All men, both as individuals and as nations, are subject to the rule of Our Lord Jesus Christ the King, and
this for two reasons. *Firstly,* because, as God, He is
our Creator. *Psalm* 32 summarizes the correct Creator-
creature relationship in the following inspired terms:

> Let all the earth fear the Lord: and let all
> the inhabitants of the world be in awe of him.
> For he spoke and they were made: he com-
> manded and they were created.

"For he spoke and they were made: he commanded
and they were created." God is our Creator. We are
His creatures. Without Him we would not exist. We
owe Him everything, and He owes us nothing. Those
who are created have an *absolute* obligation to love
and serve their Creator. This obligation is unquali-
fied; there are no "ifs," no "buts," and, as we shall
see, no question of any possible *right* on the part of
any man at any time to withhold his obedience.

It is only when men live their lives within the correct perspective of the Creator-creature relationship
that social and political harmony and order prevail.
"The peace of Christ in the Kingdom of Christ." When
men repudiate this relationship, disharmony and disorder take over, the disharmony and disorder of sin,
the disharmony and disorder introduced for the first
time into the whole of creation when the Archangel

Lucifer, the most magnificent of all God's creatures, was overcome with pride and boasted: *Non serviam*—"I will not serve." The Catechism teaches us that our purpose in life is to know, love, and serve God in this world so that we can be happy with Him forever in the next. We cannot claim to love God if we do not serve Him, and we cannot claim to serve God if we do not subject ourselves to the law of Christ the King. "If you love me," He warned, "keep my commandments." (*John* 14:15).

In *Quas Primas,* Pope Pius XI explains the second reason that we must subject ourselves to Our Lord. He explains the beautiful and profound truth that Christ is our King by acquired, as well as by natural right, for He is our Redeemer. "Would that those who forget what they have cost our Saviour," the Pope admonished us, "might recall the words: 'You were not redeemed with corruptible things, but with the Precious Blood of Christ, as of a lamb unspotted and undefiled.' We are no longer our own, for Christ has purchased us 'with a great price'; our very bodies are the 'members of Christ.'"

The double claim of Our Lord Jesus Christ to our allegiance, as our Creator and our Redeemer, is well summarized in the Book of the Apocalypse, where St. John tells us that Christ is "the ruler of the kings of the earth." (*Apoc.* 1:5). The fact that the kings of the earth—in other words, the nations and those who rule them—are subject to the Kingship of Christ pertains to what is known as His *Social Kingship,* that is, His right to rule over societies as well as individuals.

THE SOCIAL KINGSHIP OF CHRIST

No one claiming to be a Christian would, one hopes, dispute the fact that as individuals we must submit ourselves to the rule of Christ the King, but very few Christians, Catholics included, and conservative Catholics among them, understand, let alone uphold, the Social Kingship of Our Lord Jesus Christ. This is an attitude which is very common among certain well-known politicians in the United States who, while claiming to be Catholics, state with apparent pride that they do not permit their private beliefs to impinge upon their public duties. They uphold with apparent certainty the principle of the separation of Church and State. (This is a very strange attitude for a Catholic to take, but some of these politicians appear to be very strange Catholics.)

The separation of Church and State was condemned unequivocally by the Roman Pontiffs until the Second Vatican Council. The Church's teaching is that the State has an obligation to render public worship to God in accord with the teachings of the True Church, the Catholic Church, and positively to *aid* the Catholic Church in the carrying out of her functions. The State does not have the right to remain neutral regarding religion, much less to pursue a secular approach in its policies. A secular approach is by that very fact an anti-God and an anti-Christ approach. This unequivocal teaching was summarized very clearly by Pope St. Pius X, who, in his encyclical *Vehementer Nos,* condemned the principle of the separation of Church and State as "an absolutely false and most pernicious thesis."

The practical consequences of this Catholic teaching are difficult to imagine for those of us who have known nothing but a secular state, in which the State claims to have no responsibilities in matters of religion and morality. (The secular state outlaws certain immoral acts, not because they are immoral, but because the majority wish them outlawed.) Nevertheless, we must admit that this claim of the secular state is profoundly wrong.

The only word adequate to describe the claim by a Catholic politician that he will not allow his private beliefs to impinge upon his public duties is blasphemy—or at least open rebellion against God. For the Commandments of God are binding in public as well as in private, and it is blasphemous for a Christian to maintain the contrary.

The Commandment "Thou shalt not kill" precludes the taking of innocent human life. We can take another human life only as an act of self-defense, to save our lives, those of our families or friends or our fellow citizens against an unjust aggressor; but never, never, never, does any human being have the right to take the life of an innocent person. Unborn infants certainly come into this category, a fact stated forcefully, courageously, and unambiguously by our Holy Father Pope John Paul II in his encyclical letter *Centesimus Annus* of 1 May 1991, commemorating the centenary of Pope Leo XIII's encyclical *Rerum Novarum*. May God bless him for it.

Who could be more innocent of aggressive intent than an unborn child within the womb of his mother? Who could be more clearly protected by God's absolute prohibition against taking the life of the innocent than an unborn child within the womb of his mother?

What exactly is a politician such as Governor Cuomo claiming when he states that he is personally against abortion but that, as a politician, he must respect the right of a woman to murder her unborn baby? He is basing this alleged right on the fact that it has been "granted" by the law of the United States, just as it has been granted by the governments of almost every country in the Western World. In other words—and I am sure that Governor Cuomo would not dispute this—he believes that a right is acquired when it is accorded by the majority of citizens within a state. In believing this, he has accepted, in place of the Social Kingship of Our Lord Jesus Christ, and His right to rule over societies as well as individuals, the abominable theory of democracy enshrined in the French Revolution's *Declaration of the Rights of Man,* the declaration which constituted a formal and insolent repudiation of the Social Kingship of Our Lord Jesus Christ, the declaration which enshrined the greatest heresy of modern times, perhaps of all times: that authority resides in the people. On the contrary, as the Popes have taught, *Omnis potestas a Deo*—"All authority comes from God."

"Not so!" reply the revolutionaries. *Omnis potestas a populo*—"All authority comes from the people."

How well the term "revolutionaries" applies to these

men! A revolution is best defined as the forcible overthrow of an established government, and this is precisely what they did. They overthrew the Social
Kingship of Our Lord Jesus Christ in favor of what
is rightly termed the *heresy* that authority resides in
the will of the majority—the heresy that is the source
of all the evils in society today.

THE RISE OF A HERESY:
AUTHORITY COMES FROM THE PEOPLE

It would be a mistake to imagine that the dethronement of Our Lord began at the end of the 18th
Century with the promulgation by the French Revolutionaries of the so-called "Rights of Man." The process began four centuries earlier, in 14th-century Italy,
during what has become known as the "Renaissance."
The word is French and means "rebirth." It refers
to the rebirth of classical studies which began in Italy
in the 14th Century. Those engaged in these studies
were known as "humanists" because their studies were
concerned with purely human topics, whereas in Europe, until that time, God had been the focus for almost every aspect of scholarship and art. Music,
architecture, literature, painting, drama, philosophy,
cosmology and, above all, theology—the Queen of
the Sciences—were centered upon the Creator, and
the Creator-creature relationship was axiomatic to
every aspect of human thought.

Initially, there was no conflict between Humanism
and the Church. Many humanists were also ecclesias-

tics. But as time passed, it became clear that the movement was tending to relegate religion to a place where it had little or no influence on human thought or human behavior. This tendency was implicit rather than explicit. It gave rise to the attitude that whereas faith is valid in its own domain, *reason* should be concerned only with what is scientifically demonstrable. The Creator-creature relationship was not formally denied, but attention became focused almost exclusively on man, to the neglect of God, who was, effectively, confined to the sacristy. Man was seen as an autonomous being, the focus of truth in a world of which he was master and which he had the ability to subdue and perfect, a being capable of building an earthly paradise by his own efforts, a utopia. The extent to which these ideas were reflected in the principles of the French Revolution, and later in atheistic Communism, hardly needs pointing out.

The practical result of Humanism was the divinization of man. The more God was diminished, the more man exalted himself and became his own God. In his book *Christian Humanism* Professor Thomas Molnar provides us with the following definition: "Humanism was a doctrine, or network of doctrines, putting man in place of God, and endowing him with features that he was inevitably to abuse."[1]

I have mentioned the extent to which the principles of Humanism reached their logical conclusion in the French Revolution and in Communism, but the Protestant Reformation cannot be exempted from this charge. Our Lord Jesus Christ founded a visible

Church, His Mystical Body, to continue His mission in the world until He comes again in glory. This Church was endowed with a visible head, the Bishop of Rome, the Vicar of Jesus Christ. A vicar is a person who is authorized to perform a function on behalf of another, as his officially designated deputy. The Bishop of Rome has the authority to teach infallibly the true meaning of the Scriptures as intended by their Divine Author.

The Protestant Reformers repudiated the authority of the Vicar of Christ, and hence the authority of Christ Himself. They claimed to accept the authority of the Scriptures, but the inevitable logic of Protestantism is that they accept the authority of Scripture *as each individual Protestant interprets it.* In other words, every Protestant makes his own reason his ultimate authority in religious matters. It has often been said that, in the final analysis, every Protestant is his own pope. We can go further still and state that in the final analysis Protestantism makes each Protestant into his own god. This is Humanism with a vengeance.

Catholics did not, of course, remain free from these influences, and in 1907, in the fifth year of his pontificate, Pope St. Pius X felt obliged to promulgate his encyclical letter *Pascendi Dominici Gregis,* condemning the errors of that Protestantized version of Catholicism known as Modernism, the ultimate logic of which, explained the Pope, was atheism.

The most deplorable example of man's self-deification in our day is man's arrogation to himself of God's supreme and most fundamental authority, that is, His authority over life and death.

"I," says contemporary man, "shall decide for myself when a new human life shall begin and, once it has begun, whether it shall continue or be terminated. I shall use contraception to ensure that no new life is conceived without my consent, and, should a conception take place that I deem inconvenient, I shall terminate it by abortion." The next step in this diabolical process will be the legalization of euthanasia.

Although I have said that it would be a mistake to imagine that the dethronement of Christ the King was inaugurated by the promulgation of the French Revolution's *Declaration of the Rights of Man,* there can be no doubt that this Declaration constituted the first formal repudiation of Our Lord's Social Kingship, and that it was the most influential act in the process of securing His virtually universal dethronement during the next two centuries.

Before examining the extent to which this Declaration constituted a repudiation of Catholic teaching on the authority of the State, it is necessary to have a clear grasp of the content of this teaching. The doctrine of the Popes on the authority of the State is clear and self-evident to those with a proper understanding of the Creator-creature relationship, which is fundamental to a well-ordered society.

THE CHURCH AND DEMOCRACY

A state is composed of two elements: the government, or those who govern, and the governed, authority being vested in those who govern. The Church is not committed to any particular form of government, and despite the tendency of Popes to refer to "princes" in their encyclicals, they were in no way opposed to democracy, if all that is meant by this term is that those who govern are chosen by a vote (based on either limited or universal suffrage). What the Popes maintain, logically and uncompromisingly, is that the source of authority is precisely the same in an absolute monarchy, such as that of Louis XIV in 18th-century France, as in a country where the government is chosen in a democratic election in which every citizen has the right to vote, such as the United States today. In either situation papal teaching on the source of authority is clear and has already been stated: *Omnis potestas a Deo*—"All authority comes from God." Pope Leo XIII explained in his encyclical *Immortale Dei* that:

> Every civilized community must have a ruling authority, and this authority, no less than society itself, has its source in nature, and has, consequently, God for its author. *Hence it follows that all public power must proceed from God. FOR GOD ALONE IS THE TRUE AND SUPREME LORD OF THE WORLD. Everything without exception must be subject to Him, and must serve Him, so that whosoever holds the right to govern, holds it from one sole and single source, namely, God, the Sovereign Ruler of all. "There is no power but from God."* (Rom. 13:1).

"There is no power but from God." This quotation from Romans 13:1 states all that needs to be stated concerning the source of authority. Because those who govern derive their authority from God, and govern as His legates, and not as holding their authority from the people, no government can have a true right to enact any legislation contrary to the law of God, *even if such legislation is the manifest wish of the majority of the people.* The Church is totally opposed to any concept of democracy in which authority is said to reside in the people and in which those who govern are said to receive their authority from the people. Pope Leo XIII insisted in *Immortale Dei* that:

> In a society grounded upon such maxims, all government is nothing more nor less than the will of the people; and the people, being under the power of itself alone, is alone its own ruler . . . The authority of God is passed over in silence, just as if there were no God; or as if He cared nothing for human society; or as if men, in their individual capacity or bound together in social relations, owed nothing to God; or as if there could be a government *of which the whole origin and power and authority did not reside in God Himself.* Thus, as is evident, a state becomes nothing but a multitude, which is its own master and ruler.

THE DECLARATION OF THE RIGHTS OF MAN

Few English-speaking Catholics are familiar with the French Revolution's *Declaration of the Rights of Man* or with its background. The Rights of Man were discussed by the French National Assembly during the meetings of August, 1789 and adopted in October of the same year. Some of the articles are not simply acceptable but actually commendable, e.g., Article 7, concerning the detention of citizens; Article 8, stating that laws cannot have a retroactive effect; and Article 9, concerning those who have been arrested but whose guilt has not been proven. Other articles are ambiguous. But some others are positively incompatible with Catholicism, particularly Article 6, which begins by stating that the law is the expression of the general will. This is a complete negation of the teaching of the Church that all authority comes from God. Pope Pius VI had no hesitation in condemning the Declaration as "contrary to religion and to society."[2] Acceptance of the Declaration of the Rights of Man rules out the possibility of a Catholic state and the social reign of Christ the King. This is hardly surprising in view of the Masonic origin of the Declaration. Father Denis Fahey wrote:

> That the preparation and the triumph of the French Revolution were the work of Freemasonry does not need proof since the Masons themselves boast of it. Accordingly, *The Declaration of the Rights of Man* is a Masonic production.[3]

Father Fahey quoted in support of this contention a statement by Monsieur Bonnet, the orator at the Grand Orient Assembly in 1904:

> Freemasonry had the supreme honor of giving to humanity the chart which it had lovingly elaborated. It was our Brother, de la Fayette, who first presented the project of a declaration of the natural rights of the man and the citizen living in society, to be the first chapter of the Constitution. On 25 August 1789 the Constituent Assembly, of which more than 300 members were Masons, definitively adopted, almost word for word, in the form determined upon in the Lodges, the text of the immortal *Declaration of the Rights of Man*.[4]

Father Fahey summarized the Declaration as a formal renunciation of allegiance to Christ the King, of the supernatural life, and of membership in Christ's Mystical Body. He continued:

> The French State thereby officially declared that it no longer acknowledged any duty to God through Our Lord Jesus Christ, and no longer recognized the dignity of membership of Christ in its citizens. It thus inaugurated the attack on the organization of society under Christ the King which has continued down to the present day.[5]

The principle that all authority comes from the people is now all but universally accepted throughout the West. The basis of public morality is whatever the contemporary consensus of citizens is prepared to accept. It would be very hard to convince the average Catholic today that his country should not be governed by the will of the people or that our elected representatives are anything more than delegates of the people who voted them into power.

WHAT IS A "RIGHT"?

In his encyclical letter *Tametsi futura,* published in 1900, Pope Leo XIII commented: "The people have heard quite enough about what are called the rights of man. Let them hear about the rights of God for once." This is precisely what we shall do now.

Strictly speaking, God alone has rights which belong to Him of His very nature. As human beings we possess only contingent rights, rights which are accorded to us by God. We have a right to do only what is pleasing to God. This is synonymous with stating that we are free to do only what is pleasing to God, and the freedom referred to here is moral freedom, or moral liberty. Whenever the term "right" is used in this study, it must be taken to mean "moral freedom." To state that a man has a right to perform an action means that he is morally free to do so, and he can never be morally free to perform any act that is displeasing to God.

The fundamental meaning of the word "liberty" is the ability to act without constraint. There can be three forms of constraint: physical, psychological, and moral.

Freedom from physical restraint simply means the absence of any external constraint which could prevent a person from carrying out a desired action. A football player who wished to take part in an important match, but who had broken his leg and was in hospital at the time of the game, would not be physically free, or able, to participate in the event.

Psychological liberty is better known as free will and involves the capacity to make moral choices. It is thus restricted to angels and to men. Beings who possess free will, or psychological liberty, are the masters of their acts, and hence are responsible for them. Animals have physical but not psychological freedom. A pair of blackbirds necessarily selects the tree in which they will build their nest on the basis of which tree seems most useful; they cannot choose to sacrifice the better tree and select a poorer one. Nor do they possess the free will enabling them to decide *whether or not* to build a nest and raise a family, or even what type of nest to build.

It should be clear that being *physically* able to perform an action, and being *psychologically* able to choose whether to perform it, do not mean that one has a *right* to perform it. There may be a *moral* constraint against performing the action. Two simple examples should make this clear. A bank clerk might find himself in a position to defraud his employers of a large sum of money with very little likelihood of being detected. He would be physically free to per-

form the action, that is, he would be able to remove
the money without being detected. He would be psychologically free to perform it, that is, he would be
able to use, or rather misuse, his free will to commit
the theft. But he would not be *morally* free to steal
the money, since theft is forbidden by the Commandments of God. In this case the law of God and the
law of the State concur, and just as there is no moral
right to steal, there is also no legal right to steal.

But a legal right does not necessarily confer a moral
right, as the following example will demonstrate. A
woman may be physically, psychologically, and legally
free to have an abortion, but the so-called legal right
to murder her baby does not confer a true right, since
murder is forbidden by the Commandments of God.

CIVIL LAW AND THE ETERNAL LAW

In his essay *The Church and the Modern State,* published in 1931 and referring specifically to the United
States, Hilaire Belloc noted that laws declared invalid
by the Catholic Church are not binding. He continued:
"Where there is a conflict between the civil law and
the moral law of the Catholic Church, members of
the Catholic Church will resist the civil law and obey
the law of the Church."[6]

At the risk of being repetitious, I will state once
more that the teaching of the Church is that the terms
"right" and "moral liberty" are synonymous. We can
speak of a "right" only when its object is morally
licit. The Popes, Pope Leo XIII in particular, taught

time and time again that there can only be a true right—that is, the moral liberty—to choose that which is good and true. No human being can ever have a right to choose what is evil or false. To quote Pope Leo XIII, writing in *Libertas humana*:

> The true liberty of human society does not consist in every man doing what he pleases, for this would simply end in turmoil and confusion, and bring on the overthrow of the State: *but rather in this,* that through the injunctions of the civil law all may more easily conform to the prescriptions of the ETERNAL LAW.

The teaching of Pope Leo XIII is, then, that the purpose of civil law in any state, Catholic or non-Catholic, should be to assist its citizens to conform to the prescriptions of the eternal law. However, today the laws of Great Britain and the United States are designed—I repeat, *designed*—to have precisely the opposite effect. The laws of both countries incite each and every citizen to imitate Lucifer and to say: *Non serviam*—"I will not serve."

The average citizen, and this is not hard to understand, equates what is *legally* permissible with what is *morally* permissible. Let us take divorce as an example. In Great Britain the figure for divorce is around 30% and rising, and the reason that it is not rising far faster is due to the fact that such a high proportion of couples now live together without even the formality of a civil ceremony. In the U.S.A., I understand that the divorce rate is now in the region of 50%. If the law did not sanction divorce and remarriage, the number of those who would abandon their spouses to live in new unions that would be legally as well as morally illicit would be reduced to a very small fraction of this figure.

The same can be said in the matter of abortions. If abortion had not been made legal, millions of women who have had abortions would not have done so, and, as is almost invariably the case, would have loved and cherished the babies they have murdered.

Pope Leo XIII insisted in *Libertas humana* that:

> The binding force of human laws is in this, that they are to be regarded as applications of the eternal law, as in the principle of all law. . . *WHERE A LAW IS ENACTED CONTRARY TO REASON, OR TO THE ETERNAL LAW, OR TO SOME ORDINANCE OF GOD, OBEDIENCE IS UNLAWFUL, LEST WHILE OBEYING MAN WE BECOME DISOBEDIENT TO GOD.*

Can these words not be considered a charter for the Rescue Movement? We are forbidden to obey any law that is contrary to the eternal law of God, lest while obeying man, we become disobedient to God.

This unequivocal papal teaching certainly has grave implications for any Catholic involved in the enforcement of the law. By what right can a Catholic policeman arrest those who try to rescue the unborn from abortion? By what right can a Catholic district attorney prosecute them? By what right can a Catholic judge convict them? Let such public officials not protest that they have sworn to uphold the law, because any human law contrary to the eternal law cannot be considered valid by any Catholic. But, alas, many, perhaps most, Catholics holding public office today are certainly not worthy of the glorious title of Catholic.

I quoted Hilaire Belloc earlier as stating that when there is a conflict between civil law and the moral law of the Catholic Church, members of the Catholic Church will resist the civil law and obey the law of the Church. Belloc was somewhat naive in believing this since, alas, now that precisely such a conflict has arisen in the United States with the emergence of the Rescue Movement, the overwhelming majority of Catholics involved in enforcing an immoral civil law have preferred to uphold that law rather than endanger their livelihood.

REACTION TO *QUAS PRIMAS*

When Pope Pius XI promulgated *Quas Primas* in 1925, Christ the King had, to all intents and purposes, been dethroned throughout what was once referred to as Christendom. In October, 1941, in an article in *The Dublin Review,* Christopher Dawson described Europe as a secularized Christendom, its character having been largely destroyed by 200 years of secularization. "The resultant culture," he wrote, "the culture of the Liberal 19th century and of western democracy, may be described as post-Christian, i.e., it was built on Christian foundations and Christian values, but it was divorced from an organic union with Christian faith and practice.''

When he wrote *Quas Primas,* Pope Pius XI had no illusions concerning the state of what had once been Christendom. He anticipated Christopher Dawson's analysis in the opening paragraph of the encyclical, noting that the manifold evils of the world are due to the exclusion of Jesus Christ and His holy law from the private lives of individuals and from the political life of almost every state.

It was the insistence of the Pope upon the social reign of Christ the King—on the fact that states, as well as individuals, must submit themselves to His rule—which caused such embarrassment to the bishops of the world (and nowhere more so than in the United States), which has resulted, as Hamish Fraser expressed it, in *Quas Primas'* becoming the greatest non-event in the history of the Church.

LIBERTY OF CONSCIENCE?

We are all familiar with the saying that ''Everyone has the *right* to his own opinion.'' It is not unusual to hear a Catholic state that while he disagrees with the beliefs of a member of another religion, he would give his life to defend that person's *right* to hold these beliefs. I would be surprised if most Catholics today did not agree with these sentiments, but they are both untrue and reflect the classic Liberal position on liberty of conscience, which has been condemned frequently and forcefully by the Popes.

Pope Leo XIII warned in *Libertas humana* that there are certain so-called liberties which modern society takes for granted that every man possesses as a right. These are the liberties, the Pope explained, "which the followers of Liberalism so eagerly advocate and proclaim."

WHAT IS LIBERALISM?

The essence of Liberalism is the view that the individual human being has the right to decide for himself the norms by which he will regulate his life; that he has the right to be his own arbiter as to what is right and what is wrong; and that he is under no obligation to submit himself to any external authority. In the Liberal sense, "liberty of conscience" is the right of an individual to think and believe whatsoever he wants, even in religion and morality. He has the right to choose any religion, or to have no religion; and he has the right to express his views publicly and to persuade others to adopt them, using word of mouth, the public press, or any other means.

A dramatic and depressing instance of this Liberal thesis being translated into practice is the campaign for so-called "Gay Rights" in the United States and in Great Britain. Here with a vengeance are so-called "liberties," which modern society takes for granted that every man possesses as a right. In the United States you are witnessing the scarcely credible spectacle of

Catholic bishops taking it for granted that homosexuals have a right to indulge in and to propagandize in favor of their unnatural vice, and even, in some cases, helping them actively in their campaign. In Connecticut in 1991 a so-called "Gay Rights Bill" was passed, primarily due to the support of the Catholic Bishops in that state. The bill even allows homosexuals to adopt or to become foster parents of young children. Dom Prosper Guéranger wrote, at a time when such an act on the part of Catholic bishops would have been unthinkable, that when the shepherd becomes a wolf, the flock has a right to defend itself. There cannot be the least doubt that the faithful in Connecticut need to defend themselves against wolves masquerading under the guise of Catholic bishops.

IF CHRIST IS DETHRONED, WE BECOME INHUMAN

Dozens of books have been written examining the contemporary crisis within the Church from an orthodox Catholic standpoint. Among the two or three that should definitely be owned by every Catholic who loves his faith is *The Devastated Vineyard* by Dietrich von Hildebrand. In this book the author lamented the terrible decline of humanity, which is nearing the point of actual dehumanization. He stated that it is the superhuman task of the holy Church to save humanity, or at least her own children, from this downfall. I was interested to note that this great book was written in 1973, and that since that date 25 million unborn children have become the victims of legalized murder in the United States alone, and this slaughter is continuing at the rate of 4,300 a day. Was not Professor von Hildebrand right to refer to what he termed "this apocalyptic decline of humanity," which is nearing the point of actual dehumanization?[7] What other word but "dehumanized" will do for a society which extends its protection to sexual perverts and withdraws it from unborn children so that they can be massacred by the million? Christ the King has indeed been dethroned, and the evil fruits of Liberalism can be seen everywhere around us.

Professor von Hildebrand warned that the Church can only help mankind to draw back from the precipice upon which it is poised "if the vineyard of the Lord blossoms anew. And therefore we must storm Heaven with the prayer that the spirit of St. Pius X might once again fill the hierarchy, that the great words *anathema sit* might once again ring out against all heretics, and especially against all the members of the 'fifth column' within the Church."[8] We could do no better than begin by praying that they will ring out in Connecticut.

THE FEAST OF CHRIST THE KING

Pope Pius XI instituted the Feast of the Kingship of Christ to be observed by the whole world on the last Sunday of the month of October. The Proper of that Mass, and even more so the Breviary Office, contained frequent references to the Social Kingship of Our Lord Jesus Christ. The Pope explained that the annual celebration of the Feast would remind nations that not only private individuals but also rulers and princes are bound to give public honor and obedience to Christ.

This would certainly not be the case since Vatican II, as the Mass and Office for this feast have been systematically purged of every reference to Our Lord's Social Kingship. References have either been removed completely or replaced by references to our duty to subject ourselves to Christ the King *as individuals*. This is an interesting example of the principle *lex orandi, lex credendi,* which means, roughly, that what is in the liturgical texts corresponds with what we believe. Furthermore, the Feast has been transferred from the end of October to the end of November, to the end of the liturgical year. This is a change of considerable significance. Archbishop Lefebvre explained:

> During October the liturgical year is not over and three or four Sundays remain. This signifies the reign of Our Lord over time, over peoples, over all nations. The feast has been transferred to the end of the liturgical year. What does this signify? That Our Lord will reign— certainly He will, oh yes! certainly...He will reign—but at the end of time. Not now. Now, it is impossible.
>
> I will be accused of exaggerating. No; I do not exaggerate. I am sorry to have to say this. Why? Because I heard it directly from the mouth of a papal nuncio to whom I said: "You are

in the process of suppressing all the Catholic States. You have collaborated in their suppression." Then I asked the Nuncio: "And what will you do about the social reign of Our Lord Jesus Christ?" He replied: "That is no longer possible today." That is what a nuncio told me, the representative of our Holy Father the Pope. "The social reign of Christ the King is no longer possible today."

TO RESTORE THE REIGN OF CHRIST

We *must* make the social reign of Christ the King possible today. If we do not do all that is in our power to restore the Social Kingship of Our Lord, we are not worthy of our Baptism, we are not worthy of our Confirmation, we are not worthy of the glorious name of Catholic. There is only one solution to the problems of mankind, and that is to establish the peace of Christ in the Kingdom of Christ—*Pax Christi in regno Christi*. There is no other solution to what Professor von Hildebrand rightly termed the dehumanization of mankind.

Hilaire Belloc explained that the two alternatives for our civilization are Catholicism and chaos. Anything less than Catholicism—even if it calls itself "Christianity"—will not stand up in the long run against the encroaching barbarism. So it is we Catholics who actually hold the key both to the social reign of Christ and to the saving of our civilization. We must therefore all work toward the day when the governments of our nations (as well as all individual men) publicly recognize Christ, His Catholic Church and His holy law—and regulate themselves accordingly.

How is this to be achieved? If we wait for a lead from the hierarchy, it will not be given. The laity must take the lead and shame the hierarchy into following us.

Do *not* say that this cannot be done. It has been done with the fight for the Tridentine Mass, which is now being celebrated throughout the world to an extent that few of us would have deemed possible a few years ago. It has been done with the pro-life movement, above all with the Rescue Movement. We now have bishops participating in Rescues, God bless them for it. But they are following the lead of the laity.

During the Protestant Reformation, almost all the clergy in England accepted the new religion without protest until, in the West of England, they were forced to return to the traditional Faith and the traditional Mass by relatively uneducated peasants. The fact that one reluctant priest was cut to pieces with agricultural implements seems to have given his confrères considerable encouragement in returning to the Catholic Faith! Hamish Fraser insisted frequently and forcefully that society, the social kingdom of Our Lord, is our milieu as laymen, and that we must make our presence felt. Hamish Fraser was a convert from Communism, and the great legacy which he brought from his Communist background was his commitment to action.

We can fight for the Social Kingship of Our Lord

without the need of approval or leadership from our bishops. We can and must mobilize all citizens of good will, whether they are Catholic or not. There were Protestants and even Jews who fought the "Gay Rights Bill" in Connecticut, and they were undermined by our bishops.

If anyone reading this honestly believes that society cannot be changed, I can only reply: "Tell that to the homosexuals, tell that to the abortionists." They *have* changed society, they have corrupted it, dehumanized it, but they knew what they wanted and they were prepared to fight for it, and they are still prepared to fight for it. Shall the children of light show less zeal than the children of darkness?

Rather than offer a plan of detailed suggestions for action, which limitations of space would not permit in any case, I will appeal to all Catholics to subscribe to *The Remnant*. It is a serious journal with a serious purpose for serious people.* We can use it to inform ourselves and to motivate ourselves into launching a crusade to restore the Social Reign of Christ the King in our neighborhoods and in our countries.

This is a providential moment to begin this crusade. There is a definite revulsion among basically decent people at what they see happening to society, and, as Catholics, we can mobilize them to campaign against so-called "rights" which, as I hope that I have demonstrated in this study, are not rights at all, and

---

*Write for subscription details to 2539 Morrison Avenue, St. Paul, MN 55117, U.S.A.

cannot be rights, because they are contrary to the law of Christ the King.

Let us begin the campaign to restore our King to His rightful throne by working to overthrow the diabolic trinity of abortion, pro-homosexual legislation, and pornography. These are evils that cry to Heaven for vengeance. They were not legal when we were children, and they can be made illegal once again.

''Impossible,'' you may say. Why impossible? Impossible because we, as the children of light, are not as prepared to commit ourselves to the fight for what is good as the children of darkness are to commit themselves to the fight for what is evil?

Because all men are subject to the law of Christ the King, particularly in what concerns the natural law, which is engraved in the heart of every human being, we must, as I have just suggested, do all in our power to enlist the support of both Catholic and non-Catholic people in the fight for those basic decencies which are absolutely essential to the social reign of Christ and without which society will disintegrate. As Professor von Hildebrand has warned us, we shall even become dehumanized. Would any reader deny that if an American Catholic wishes to seek inspiring leadership in the fight to uphold the fundamental moral principles of our faith, he is more likely to find it by listening to Senator Jesse Helms than to 99% of the so-called Catholic bishops?

Although few Protestants could articulate the doctrine of Christ's Kingship in the formal manner that it is explained in *Quas Primas,* many of them believe and profess it almost by instinct. The outstanding pro-life journal in the English-speaking world is certainly *The Rescuer* (P.O. Box 320, Drexel Hill, PA 19026). In its September, 1991 issue it republished an article from a secular journal concerning the historic 1991 Rescue in Wichita. The report began with an account of the action and the words of a Protestant lady. There is an obvious contrast between this lady's stand and that of virtually all the English-speaking bishops of the post-conciliar era. There could be no testimony more eloquent to the abysmal state to which Holy Mother Church has been reduced in our countries.

The following report is from Wichita, Kansas:

WICHITA, KANSAS—Pam Schuffert stood at the barricades, a hefty woman in overalls stitched in neon colors with admonitions from Proverbs, holding in one hand a copy of an order from U.S. District Judge Patrick F. Kelly.

In the other hand she clutched the worn leather-bound Bible she has carried in previous protests and during the 150 days she has spent in jail since taking up a fervent defense of the unborn.

"We'll obey the laws of man when we can," she declared into the loudspeaker, waving Kelly's order, "but we have to obey the laws of God. God's word shall stand over every earthly judge. We say *this* judge stands in contempt of a higher judge."

"We say this judge stands in contempt of a higher judge." Could Pope Leo XIII have expressed the doctrine of Christ the King more clearly? And alas, the judge that she indicted for being in contempt of a higher judge, Judge Patrick F. Kelly, claims to be a Catholic! What, one wonders, would Hilaire Belloc have thought of this? "Where," he wrote, "there is a conflict between civil law and the moral law of the Catholic Church, members of the Catholic Church will resist the civil law and obey the law of the Church." Yet, here we have a so-called Catholic judge who is not simply ready but eager to imprison Protestants who uphold the law of God as taught by his own Church, a law which he looks upon with total contempt.

On 25 October 1991 I watched a program on BBC TV concerning the crusade against pornography by an American lady named Andrea Dworkin. She quoted statistics to the effect that today one in three girls in the United States is subjected to sexual abuse within her home. Can Dietrich von Hildebrand be accused of exaggeration in speaking of the dehumanization of contemporary society? Andrea Dworkin claimed that pornography plays a significant role in the explosion of child abuse, and I am sure that she is correct. I was interested—and saddened—to note that she did not invoke the name of God even once during the entire program. Her opposition to pornography was based entirely on the fact that it is a violation of women's rights—which is perfectly true. But, as I explained earlier, all human rights are contingent; they exist only because they are accorded to us by Christ the King. What was most interesting in her argumentation was her attack upon the so-called "free speech" protected by the First Amendment to the American Constitution: "The golden rule in the United States," she stated, "is that we must have free speech." But Andrea Dworkin went on to explain in the most articulate manner that there are values which must take precedence over free speech. Even from a secular perspective, she could see that rights are not absolute. But I am afraid that many English-speaking bishops would not agree with her.

Hamish Fraser was very fond of quoting Edmund Burke's dictum that for the triumph of evil it is only necessary that good men do nothing. If we do nothing, can we even call ourselves "good men"?

"Christ is the ruler of the kings of the earth" and He must reign: *Opportet illum regnare.* It is to be hoped that many will follow the example of Hamish Fraser in dedicating their entire lives to re-establishing that reign.

OUR FIRST TASK

Dietrich von Hildebrand taught correctly that in a state consisting principally of non-Catholics it is the vocation of Catholics to act as a leaven, but how can they do this when their commitment to the Kingdom of Christ the King is, in most cases, so manifestly inferior to that of so many devout Protestants?

This means that, in re-establishing the reign of

Christ the King, our first task must be to re-evangelize the Catholic community. We must fight for orthodox religious instruction in our schools, and above all, for a liturgy in which Our Lord is recognized clearly as our King, and this must be the traditional Mass of the Roman Rite, the Tridentine Mass. The liturgy of the traditional Mass is focused upon God, that in the New Mass is focused upon the community. The reign of Christ the King cannot be established until He becomes once more the center of our lives.

Christ is the ruler of the kings of the earth and He must reign—*Opportet illum regnare.* Let us take the first and most important step in dedicating ourselves to re-establishing that reign by implementing in our own lives the requirement for prayer and penance demanded by Our Lady of Fatima. If this is done, and if Russia is consecrated to her Immaculate Heart by the Pope in union with the bishops of the world, she promised that many souls will be saved, Russia will be converted, and there will be peace. Thus her Immaculate Heart will triumph. With the triumph of the Immaculate Heart of Mary will come the re-establishment of the Kingdom of Christ the King.

I would like to conclude on a note of optimism. Our Lady has promised that, in the end, her Immaculate Heart *will* triumph. She has promised this, and she will fulfill what she has promised.

This means that without doubt her Son will reign— He *must* reign! *Opportet illum regnare.*

It is our duty and our privilege to dedicate our lives

to re-establishing this reign, to achieving the re-enthronement of Christ the King. *Opportet illum regnare.*

"He must reign! He must reign!"

NOTES

1. T. Molnar, *Christian Humanism* (Chicago, 1978), p. 29.
2. Encyclical Letter *Adeo nota,* 23 April 1791.
3. Foreword to G. Dillon, *Grand Orient Freemasonry Unmasked* (London: Britons Publishing Company—now, Chulmleigh: Augustine, 1965), p. 16.
4. Ibid., pp. 16-17.
5. Ibid., p. 17.
6. H. Belloc, *Essays of a Catholic* (London, 1931), p. 84. (This work was republished in 1992 by TAN Books and Publishers, Inc.)
7. D. von Hildebrand, *The Devastated Vineyard* (Chicago: Franciscan Herald Press, 1973), p. 52. (Reprinted by the Catholic Media Apostolate, Box 255, Harrison, N.Y. 10528, at $15.50 including postage and handling.)
8. Ibid., p. 54.

If you have enjoyed this book, consider making your next selection from among the following . . .

Prices subject to change.

Prices subject to change.

Prices subject to change.